Door of No Return

The Legend of Gorée Island

Steven Barboza

ILLUSTRATED WITH PHOTOGRAPHS

COBBLEHILL BOOKS
DUTTON   NEW YORK

ILLUSTRATION CREDITS

Anthony Barboza, 30, 31; Ronald Barboza, *vi*, 34, 36, 37; Steven Barboza, 4, 5, 8,
10, 14, 16, 17, 18, 20, 21, 22, 25, 26, 28, 29, 32, 38, 47; Societe Africaine
d'Edition, 6; Editions Clairafrique Dakar, 13. Map on page 11 by Claudia Carlson.

Library of Congress Cataloging-in-Publication Data
Barboza, Steven.
Door of no return : the legend of Gorée Island / Steven Barboza.
p.   cm.
ISBN 0-525-65188-8
1. Gorée Island (Senegal)—Description and travel—Juvenile literature.
[1. Gorée Island (Senegal)—History. 2. Slave trade—
Africa, West.] I. Title.
DT549.9.G67B37   1994   93-21163
966.3—dc20   CIP
                                AC

Published in the United States by Cobblehill Books,
an affiliate of Dutton Children's Books,
a division of Penguin Books USA Inc.
375 Hudson Street, New York, New York 10014

Designed by Sylvia Frezzolini
Printed in Hong Kong

First Edition

10 9 8 7 6 5 4 3 2 1

Dedicated to

The millions of captured Africans, whose souls survive . . .
Any visitor, African American or white or whatever, whose emotions have
been stirred in Gorée's slave dungeons . . .
Maria Nharita, who never learned much about her African ancestry . . .
My wife, my mother, and my father, whose love I return.

Acknowledgments

I wish to thank Susan Barrow for useful translations, Andrée Leopold for
valuable guidance, my editor for her good judgment and dedication to
bringing this book to print, my father for his love and support, and my wife
for her patience, warmth, and strength—and superb editorial skills.

CONTENTS

Slaves who passed through this door in the House of Slaves on Gorée Island never again saw their homeland.

INTRODUCTION

AT THE THRESHOLD

Doors open and close, and sometimes in their swing, worlds collide. The history of Gorée Island is such a case.

Gorée Island is certainly just what its name implies—an island. But for centuries it also served as a "doorway." Europeans used this "doorway" as an entry point to the mainland, about two miles away; Africans unwillingly used it as an exit from their homes. They were never to return.

Today, thousands of African Americans and European Americans visit Gorée to examine dungeons in the House of Slaves and stand in its "Door of No Return," looking out to sea. They try to understand the tragic history that brought their ancestors together. For one heart-rending moment, the pain and suffering of slavery become terribly clear. It leaves many in tears.

In a sense, the trip is a sojourn through that old doorway—this time back to Africa instead of from it. *My forefathers could not return*, some African Americans think, *so we came back for them*.

I passed through that doorway and imagined history taking shape before my eyes. I cringed, and I cried, and vowed never to let history repeat itself.

I also realized something significant about my ancestors. They were survivors. Yes, history had treated them cruelly. It separated mothers from children, husbands from wives, sisters from brothers. But shackles and hard, backbreaking work in sugarcane and cotton

1

fields in a foreign land did not shatter their spirit. The will to live still flowed in their veins. I was proud of them.

Gorée's story includes slave pens, blazing cannon, haunting spirits, African chiefs who sold prisoners of war into slavery, rebellions, a glamorous society of mixed races, and slaves who wore dazzling gold jewelry to display the wealth and status of their owners. It is a complicated, fascinating story—one that most history books ignore.

Few islands bear the stamp of their past like Gorée. Many of its walls are crumbling, but they still serve as memorials, and Gorée Islanders are reminders.

In the pages ahead, you will get a glimpse of this legendary island and its people, and will understand why its story should be known.

CHAPTER ONE

BENEATH THE CHARM

About two miles west of Dakar, the capital of Senegal, lies Gorée Island. Today, it is a Senegalese resort of seaside cafes and old homes. Government ministers vacation there. People stroll along sandy lanes and doze off at the beach, reading French magazines, making puzzles, playing games. Girls and boys dive off the seawall into the greenish clear water. Pleasure craft, moored in the harbor, are protected from the rough open sea.

The island appears quiet and quaint. And it is. But its history is marked by turbulence.

Eons ago, an underwater volcano erupted, and Gorée Island sprang violently from the ocean floor. The island lay just off the westernmost tip of Africa, a point of land that juts into the sea like a curled finger. The island was small—only 900 meters in length and 300 meters at its widest point.

One-third of Gorée is mountain. Basalt cliffs rise 300 feet above the crashing waves. The other, narrower end is just above sea level. There, on the northeastern coast, lies a calm bay.

For centuries, Africans fished near the island. The Wolof tribe of Africans called the island Ber. It was settled by a few fishermen and goatherders before Europeans stumbled onto it. In the thirteenth century, European seamen thought the ocean ended in a swirling abyss near the African coast. Portuguese explorers ventured along the coast looking for what they thought would be the end of the

A boy inspects the rocks at low tide along the seawall at Gorée Island's harbor.

Opposite: From the basalt cliffs of Gorée one can see Dakar on the mainland.

earth. What they found instead was tropical country and African societies.

PALMA

In 1444, Portuguese explorer Dinis Diaz arrived at Ber, a barren island at the time inhabited only by wild goats. He called it Palma and claimed it for the Portuguese crown. Afterward, many explorers stopped at Palma, including many mentioned in history books: Pedro Alvares Cabral, Vasco da Gama, Amerigo Vespucci. Portuguese explorer Diego d'Azemba arrived in 1482 to build a church and cemetery and trading post.

The Portuguese developed contacts on the mainland, and traded with Africans of the Jolof Empire, which included several tribes on the African mainland. From Europe, traders brought things never before seen by the Africans: gunpowder, guns, liquor, fabrics, mirrors, and jewelry. In return, the African rulers traded leather, animal skins, gold, ivory, ostrich feathers, musk, amber—and thousands of slaves. The slave trade, sometimes called the "ebony trade," thrived for

Aerial view of Gorée Island

centuries. Eventually, every major European power got involved.

As early as 1433, Africans were captured by other Africans, sold to Portuguese traders, and shipped to Lisbon, Portugal's capital. Slaves were common there by the time Columbus found the New World. The customs house in Lisbon recorded that 3,589 slaves arrived in Lisbon between 1486 and 1493. Some historians think slaves traveled with Columbus across the Atlantic. At the time, a good horse could be traded for fourteen or fifteen slaves.

From Palma, some Portuguese traders ventured deeper into Africa, where they lived in villages and acted as intermediaries, selling slaves to Europeans. Some of the Europeans even adopted local African customs, such as tattooing themselves.

Palma was cherished among European explorers and slave traders. It lay at the beginning of the shortest route from Africa to the West Indies. It was the point where the route around South Africa met the trans-Atlantic route to the Americas, and it provided safe harbor near the mainland. Over three centuries, the island changed hands among European nations seventeen times.

Ships flying the flags of Portugal, France, or Italy docked at Palma, using the island as a stopover where they could safely hold slaves for a time and resupply ships with food and caskets of fresh drinking water.

But the Portuguese, who discovered the island in 1444, established their main slave trading post 385 miles to the west, on the Cape Verde Islands, an archipelago. They found the Cape Verde Islands uninhabited in the 1460s and brought many captives there —Africans from the Mandjak, Mandinka, Fula, and Balante tribes.

Each year, the Portuguese brought 500 to 1,000 slaves to Palma before journeying on to the Cape Verde Islands, where the Africans were forced to grow sugar and maize. Before 1600, many of these slaves were re-exported to Colombia, Mexico, the Canary Islands, and Seville, Spain.

Cannon, no longer used to protect the harbor of Gorée, stand silent at Fort d'Estrées, named after the French admiral who recaptured the island from the Dutch in 1677.

CHAPTER TWO

TREASURED ISLAND

In 1619, a Dutch "man of warre" sailed to Jamestown, Virginia. Aboard were some twenty African slaves—the first to land in the English colony in North America. The ship may well have set sail from Gorée Island, starting slave shipments to England's mainland colony.

Some thirty years earlier, in 1588, the Dutch settled Gorée and built two forts: Nassau, by the shore, and Orange, on the mountain. They renamed the island *Goede Reede*, which meant "good harbor." The island became known as Gorée.

From Gorée, Europeans shipped slaves to the West Indies, and according to one historian, more than 13 percent of the slaves imported to the North American mainland were from the region of Africa near where Gorée lies.

As competition for slaves heightened, Gorée grew in value as a slave post. Wars were fought for it. In 1629, João Pereira-Corte Real, the Portuguese governor of the Cape Verde Islands, destroyed the Dutch forts. A year later, the Dutch recaptured the island. In 1645, the Portuguese and then the French seized Gorée. The Dutch retook the island two years later. The British occupied it in 1664. The Dutch regained it again. Finally, in 1677, the French drove out the Dutch permanently and kept it for most of the next two centuries. They leveled the Dutch forts and built their own, Saint-Michel and Saint-François, on the same sites.

In the 1600s and 1700s, some fifty European fortresses were built along 300 miles of the Gold Coast—the shoreline of what is today Ghana, on the Gulf of Guinea. The larger forts were called "castles." One of them, Cape Coast Castle, housed more than 1,000 slaves at a time. Slaves from there were packed like spoons, sometimes 350 to 400, aboard slave ships bound for the New World.

Gorée never housed as many slaves as Cape Coast Castle, but the island remained an active and important port from which some 60,000 slaves were delivered to the Americas, and its slave quarters are among the best-preserved.

Ships arrived on the Gold Coast and at Gorée, and were loaded with slaves for the journey to the New World. In the "triangular slave trade," European ships brought manufactured goods to the African coast to be

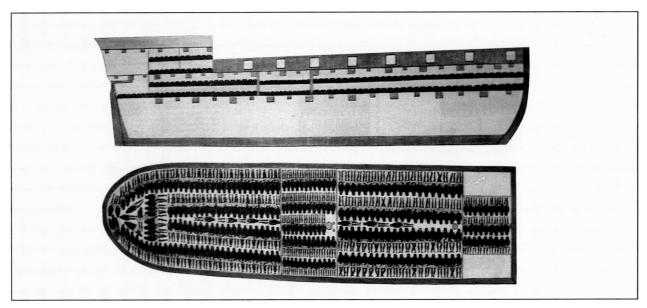

Slaves were jam-packed aboard slave ships bound for the New World.

traded for slaves. The slaves were then transported for sale in the West Indies and the Americas. Finally, the ships carried molasses and other West Indian products to Europe on the final leg of their voyage.

Accurate records were not kept, so we will never know precisely how many children of Africa became slaves. Historians say millions died on slave ships, but perhaps 10 million to 12 million Africans survived the voyages —as many people as there are living today in Illinois or Ohio or Pennsylvania. Until about 1820, for every European that came to the New World, five Africans were brought. Of the 700 million people in the New World today, one scholar estimates that about 100 million are of African ancestry.

Slavery touched every tribe in Africa, splintering families. But not every slave was shipped to the West. Many remained on the African continent. By the late 1800s, slaves made up two-thirds of many African societies.

Meanwhile, on Cape Verde, a mixed race of people emerged: Cape Verdeans. Their roots were in both Africa and Portugal. My

grandparents were Cape Verdean. Their ancestors—and, of course, mine—were probably slaves who stopped on Gorée on their way to Cape Verde.

GORÉE'S GOLDEN YEARS

In 1786, King Louis XVI of France appointed Chevalier Jean Stanislas de Boufflers commander and governor of Senegal. He lived like a king in Senegal for two years. The governor transferred his administration from Saint-Louis, the capital and port town at the mouth of the Senegal River, to Gorée, making the island the chief African port for the French navy. Gorée's population boomed to 2,000.

The island prospered as the capital of Senegal. Companies chartered in France were granted monopolies on slave trading in the region, and slaves arrived at Gorée from French trading posts along the coast or from the banks of the Senegal River. From France came weapons, iron, copper, textiles, beads, paper. In return, Gorée transshipped goods from mainland Africa, including marble for the Palace of Versailles—and slaves.

Elegant houses were built in the eighteenth century, when Gorée grew rich. The houses had verandas, orange-tiled roofs, raftered ceilings, fireplaces, airy rooms, and courtyards paved with polished basalt and a purplish-gray volcanic rock from the Canary Islands.

By day, slaves pounded basalt with cannonballs, breaking it up for building materials. They made bricks from clay. They whitewashed walls, and by night, they were crammed into the ground-floor dungeons of the stone houses they had built.

While on Gorée, the governor married "local style." His "temporary" wife was a mulatto named Anne Pepin. She was a *signare*, a member of a privileged class of Senegalese women who were the mistresses of the French and the British. Gorée's *signares* had mixed African and European blood. The name may have been derived from the Portuguese word, *senhora*, a respected woman.

Signares *were wealthy and enjoyed dressing in finery and jewelry.*

Signares were invaluable to whites because the Europeans on Gorée were ignorant about African ways of life. *Signares* translated, explained cultures, and assisted in business deals with Africans.

Eventually, *signares* developed trading networks in Africa and grew rich. European men gained access to the networks by marrying *signares* "local style"—paying a dowry to parents, sponsoring a wedding feast, remaining faithful to them, granting their name to offspring, and buying a slave to care for each child.

One *signare* lived in a beautiful stone house, which today is the island's dispensary. In 1767, she was the richest woman on Gorée. She owned sixty-eight slaves.

The *signares* displayed their wealth any chance they got. They wore loose-fitting gowns and turbans, large earrings, massive wrist and ankle bracelets, and huge gold chains draped across their bosoms. They vied for attention, walking the streets all decked out in finery, and dressed their slaves like

Victoria Albis, a celebrated signare, once owned this prow-shaped home. It now houses a museum.

mannequins in elaborate costumes and expensive jewelry. Slaves accompanied them everywhere, shading the *signares* with parasols.

Descendants of *signares* still live on Gorée. "You have a lot of *signare* families here today," a Goréan woman told me. "Some died. Some are in Dakar. *Signares* are not a bad thing. It was what they call in French the *bourgeois* Goréan."

CHAPTER THREE

THE DOOR OF NO RETURN

"My name is Anna Rosalie Faye," a Goréan woman says in imperfect yet understandable English. "I am a native of this island, and my family has been here now for eight generations. They were animists. They changed to Christian when the missionaries came here."

Anna is a typical Goréan. She's a restaurant owner and her father, Joseph N'Diaye, is the conservator of the island museum, called the House of Slaves.

Anna greets me in the courtyard of her one-level, seaside home, a few houses away from the House of Slaves. Surrounded by grandchildren and bleating goats, she is dressed exquisitely in a red-and-gold robe and gold jewelry. Her hair is bound in a turban.

We enter her living room, filled with modern furniture. As African news blares on a color television tucked into a wall unit, we sit on the sofa and talk about her family and her island.

"The Slave House is three houses from my house," she points out. "During the time of slavery, the island had a lot of slave houses, and now there is only one that the government keeps to show to the people what was slavery. This was one of many. That's the last one built—in 1776."

She says the Maison des Esclaves (House of Slaves), on Rue St.-Germain, was passed down from family to family. The last family to live there moved out in 1959.

The building was constructed by Nicholas

Pepin, whose sister was Anne Pepin, *signare* of the French governor. The House of Slaves was Nicholas's personal estate, but eventually it became a prototype for slave-trading posts. It held 400 slaves at a time.

The ground floor housed slave quarters: separate dark, dank cells for women, for children, and for men. In some cells, slaves were chained to the wall. In two cells, difficult slaves were shackled and partially submerged in salt water, causing sores. Still other cells were no bigger than four feet wide.

A passageway leads to the infamous "Door of No Return." It was said that Africans who passed through that doorway would never see Africa again. Outside that door stretched a 200-foot pier, where slave ships docked, and sharks lurked. Those slaves who could not survive the sometime three-month stay in the House of Slaves before being shipped across the Atlantic were fed to the fish.

Upstairs was luxurious by comparison. Two

Anna Rosalie Faye lives with her children and grandchildren near the House of Slaves.

Some slave dungeons housed infants separated from their mothers. The sign in French over the door reads: "Innocent child far away from the laugh and the cry of your mother."

curving stairways sloped up to the breeze-filled master's quarters with beautiful floor-boards, louvered shutters that opened onto beautiful ocean views and, at one time, fancy furnishings.

Today, the walls of the conservator's office, in the House of Slaves, are covered with photographs of famous visitors: Nelson Mandela, Harry Belafonte, Danny Glover, James Brown, Jesse Jackson, Alex Haley, Colin Powell, Robert Mogabe. A letter from Ronald Brown, U.S. Secretary of Commerce, who visited the island in 1991, reads: "Let us never forget the consequences of human deprivation."

"How does it feel to see all those black Americans go by your house to the House of Slaves?" I asked Anna.

"You know, when I see the black Americans going to the Slave House," she replied,

The Albis house has slits as air vents in rooms that once housed slaves.

"I feel that they come to see the land of their ancestors. They are right. They are pilgrims. When their ancestors were leaving, people were saying it was a one-way ticket. Maybe their ancestors did not come back, but the roots come back. You know, for a black American, that is something *very* important —to see the Slave House. To see how the slaves were kept. To see how they were suffering.

"Some visitors cry, and they say *Never this again! Never this again! Why did they do that to us? How can people do that!*" Anna exclaims. "The children in America should know the story of slavery. Maybe one day they will come to see, so they can love the other black people, the African people."

Whenever she sees black Americans visiting Gorée, she thinks of them as long-lost relatives. "You know, very often when I see them passing, I say, 'Look at this one. He looks like a Bambara. Look at this one—like a Yoruba. Very *very* much. If I look at them I can tell them exactly which tribe they belong to," says Anna, whose family is of the Serer tribe of Africa.

Other Goréans feel the same. "They look at black Americans as maybe brothers and sisters. They say, 'Oh, our brothers and sisters are here! Look at our families!' But they cannot communicate with them. They just look at them, and they are a little afraid to talk with them. We think that's a little wall, but now that is changing a lot. I remember myself, when I was younger, I was a little afraid to talk with black Americans, but that has changed," Anna says. "Now I can talk with you about slavery."

I want to get a real feel for the place—I want to sleep the night inside the House of Slaves, I tell Anna.

"Oh, don't stay in the House of Slaves!" she warns. "Most of the slave houses—they are like haunted houses."

I could not arrange to spend the night in the House of Slaves. Yet sleep in the old home of a slave owner I did.

That night, I lay with my back toward the wall and listened intently to an orchestra of crickets. It sounded deafening, seeping through the walls of a 12-foot by 10-foot room, where I was stretched out on a thin mattress. The air was still, the night pitch black. A single bare bulb hung from the ceiling. Water bugs as big as my thumb crawled on the rafters above my head.

After awhile, I finally fell asleep, but not before wondering about the lives of those who had shut their eyes in this room. If the walls in the House of Slaves had witnessed such abominable cruelties, what had happened in *this* room? Had slaves slept here, too? Or was this the bedroom of some more fortunate soul?

The door of the room opened onto the courtyard of the house that had once belonged to Anne Pepin, born in 1756—a rich and beautiful and powerful woman, wife of the governor of Senegal. She owned thirty-five slaves, and yet African blood flowed in her veins.

Anne's now-dilapidated house at 47 Rue

This doorway led to a 12-foot by 10-foot room with only a thin mattress for a bed. Had slaves slept in this room?

de Bambara (Bambara is the name of an African tribe) almost certainly has a sinister history. But it is peaceful now. You rent a room, and the proprietor, Capt. Gilbert Clermont, gives you a key to the front door. You notice that this retired seaman and descendant of Anne Pepin has tattooed arms. In the morning, he sits at the table in the courtyard overgrown with shrubbery, and as you eat French bread and sip coffee, he proudly shows you photo albums of his family. His mother was African royalty, he says, and Ethiopian Emperor Haile Selassie visited her in 1964.

He talks of how fine life was on Gorée—fishing and swimming and working and partying. His manners are kind. But you begin thinking that his house, like so many others, was not; it reeks of eeriness: slaves moaning, dreaming nightmares. With its overbearing history, this whole island is a holocaust museum. Its geography helped determine its destiny.

Capt. Gilbert Clermont holds a photograph of his mother, who claimed to be an African princess.

The sandy lanes on Gorée are cool. They have an abundance of bougainvillea.

CHAPTER FOUR

STRUGGLING TO BE FREE

Once they had their catch, slave traders of Gorée sorted slaves according to ethnic groups—Wolof, Mandinka, Serer, Fulani, Bambara, others. Then they put them in "collards"—chains five or six feet long with a flat iron collar that was clasped around the neck.

Wearing these collards, the slaves worked. They built stone buildings. They unloaded and loaded cargo. They rolled barrels of water to be stored.

And before being packed into the holds of slave ships, they were branded with the emblem of their masters, filling the air with the odor of singed flesh.

The slaves did not always take the cruelty tamely, and their stories of revolt are bone-chilling.

In October, 1724, around four o'clock in the afternoon, fifty-five slaves broke loose. Armed with sticks, knives, and axes, they attacked a guard, who screamed and alarmed others. His rescuers shot and killed two slaves and wounded twelve others. The remaining slaves ran for cover, locking themselves in a building. Guards threatened to burn the building with the slaves inside.

The slaves surrendered. Two of the ringleaders were shot on the spot. The third was quartered.

Another rebellion involved African warriors. In 1755, the King of Bawol defeated the King of Sine on the battlefield. But as the Bawolis celebrated their victory, the Sine warriors attacked again, surprising them. Bawoli generals were killed, and 500 of their warriors were taken prisoner, quickly sold and shipped to Gorée.

The warriors formed a detailed plan to escape from Gorée and return to their homeland to reclaim victory. A child overheard the plan and told it to the European commander, who assembled the prisoners in the fort and questioned the African leaders.

Yes, it is true, the leaders admitted. We planned to seize weapons and kill the guards so we could escape—not because we hate Europeans but because we wanted to return to the battlefield to regain our honor. We are ashamed not to have died fighting like brave warriors. And since our attempt has failed, we ask to be killed. *We prefer death to slavery!*

Their request was granted. A cannon was pointed at the leaders. They were shot before the other captives. The rest of the Bawoli warriors were herded aboard a vessel and shipped into slavery.

Islanders witnessed many other cruelties, and yet, ironically, during the second half of the 1800s, the island was nicknamed "Gorée the Joyous." The name today hardly seems apt, but when the French abolished house slavery and indentured servitude in 1848—the year that Senegal officially became a colony of France—freed islanders celebrated. At the time, three-quarters of the population were slaves.

Under the French, who had regained the island in 1763, considerable building was done. Captive slaves were put to work before being shipped to the New World. Buildings and houses of stone were erected; tiled roofs replaced the thatched roofs seen throughout Gorée. Shops and markets sprang up. The population soared to 5,000. Profits from the slave trade brought prosperity to Gorée.

After 1848, with Gorée's inhabitants freemen, a new era began. Schools were established and education became an important asset. Gorée's schools molded students who have changed the course of African history.

Mother Anne-Marie Javouhey, who devoted much of her life to fighting slavery, sent sisters from the order of Saint Joseph of Cluny to Gorée in 1819. They opened primary schools, and later secondary schools.

One of the most famous islanders was Blaise Diagne, born in 1872. He served in the French National Assembly and founded the first West African political party, the Republican Socialist Party of Senegal.

Modibo Keita (1915–1977), who became president of Mali, attended the William Ponty Academy, a teacher training college on Gorée. Another student, Félix Houphouët-Boigny (1905–1993), became president of the Ivory Coast in 1960.

GORÉE TODAY

About 1,500 people live on Gorée now—a far cry from a population of around 5,000 people back in 1832. Many commute by ferryboat to jobs in Dakar, Senegal's capital, two miles away. Many of Gorée's residents are members of the Toucouleur tribe, heirs of one of Senegal's earliest civilizations. They are drawn to Gorée because of its quaintness and because the ocean breezes are cool compared

Tourists stop at the church of St. Charles Borromeo, built on Gorée in 1830.

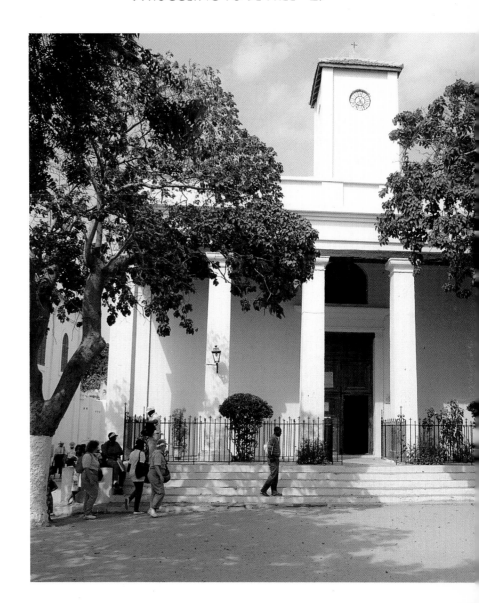

to the blazing sun on the African mainland.

Most Goréans would rather put slave history behind them. "One thing is very important," says the forty-five-year-old artist Sulaiman Keita, who was born on Gorée and whose paintings sell in Parisian art galleries. "I was born here. I was raised here. I look at the *beauty* of the island. The *background* of the island is not my business. I know the background, but I don't live it. I live for the future."

Visiting Americans have drafted plans to build a memorial on Gorée, one as big as the Statue of Liberty in New York Harbor. Some Goréans laugh about it. "Who needs it?" says Sulaiman. "The island is a museum already! The Slave House is a museum, but the *whole island* is a museum."

This "museum" is a feature attraction for tourists. A ferryboat deposits streams of them at the wharf. They visit the House of Slaves,

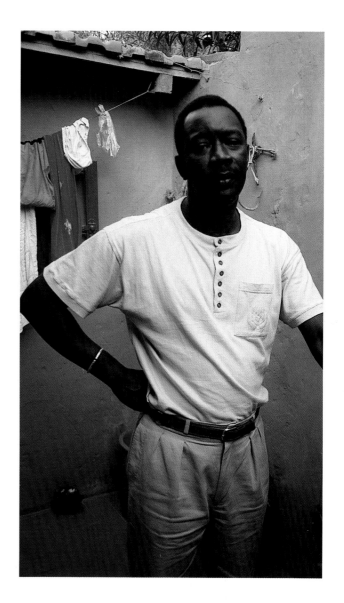

Sulaiman Keita, an artist whose works sell abroad, was raised on Gorée. He and his family still live on the island.

and take pictures of one another as they pose in the Door of No Return. They wander around the House, feeling the walls as though trying to contact spirits pent up in the cells. They peek through windows—verticle slits just wide enough to let a little air inside, yet too slim to allow slaves to climb out.

Then visitors roam the island, past acacia and mango trees, and climb the mountain to look over toward Dakar. As they walk along, many Africans attempt to sell them trinkets —symbols of a sojourn to Africa.

A vendor followed one black American from Detroit as he trudged along. "Don't you want to buy a souvenir from Gorée?" the vendor insisted.

"*I am a souvenir from Gorée!*" was the reply as the visitor refused, thinking no doubt about his ancestors, who may have been shipped from the island. He may be right.

At night, tourists return to Dakar's fancy hotels, and Gorée settles down to an even slower, island pace. Boys and girls in small groups sit in the sand and chat. Men gather around tables in cafes to watch television.

On my tour of the island, I visit a little shop to buy soda. A family of ten or more squats around a large bowl, scooping up handfuls of millet for supper.

I pass houses, mainly of basalt brick, that date from the 1700s and 1800s, built by slaves. Many are two stories—the top floor where the masters lived, and the ground floor where slaves slept.

An American's house I visit is different. It looks more like a rich rancher's estate. Nicholas Rofe, a businessman who works for an international corporation that lends money to develop private firms in Africa, decided to live on Gorée because it was quiet. He commutes to Dakar to his office.

Another American, Harriet Boyce from California, now lives on Rue de Camel in a two-story home that still has its original tile floors, laid in the 1700s. "I'm sure slaves lived here," says Harriet, lounging in her living room on the second floor. The breeze blows in through the open shutters and the door. "Every house has some place downstairs where slaves were kept.

"I came here in 1968," she continues. "It was a little paradise. There is no way to explain how beautiful this place was at that time. I was a Peace Corps volunteer—the first *toubab* (white person, in Wolof) here in many years.

"The first day I came here," she says, "I could just feel some spirit about the island that was profound. That's when I decided I would live here. I still think it's a very beautiful island. I still don't think I can find a place to live as well and peaceably as here."

Some Goréans are well known in Dakar. They are considered suburbanites, slow-paced people. "Everybody knows who lives on this island," Harriet says. "I go to Dakar and people call out, 'Hey, Madam Gorée!'"

A PARIS, A MECCA, AND A TIMBUKTU

In the old days, Africans spent more than a month at sea, jam-packed in the bowels of slave ships voyaging to the New World. To-

Harriet Boyce, from California, has lived on the island for many years.

day, many African Americans make the return trip, from New York City, in little more than seven hours via jumbo jet. They land at Dakar's international airport and take a 22-minute ferryboat ride to Gorée.

For many, Dakar offers the first glimpse of African civilization. It is called the "gateway to black Africa," as well as the "Paris of Africa." Dakar is filled with wondrous sights and sounds and smells. It is an amalgam of competing black African, Islamic, and French influences, evident on a stroll around town.

The ferryboat from Dakar brings tourists to Gorée and carries islanders to jobs in the city.

On sidewalks, boys—and grown men—hold hands as they walk down the streets. It is an African gesture of friendship and brotherhood.

People eat African-style. Three or four men sit on low stools, or boxes, around bowls of *cheboudienne*, the one-pot meal chock-full of fish and vegetables. They dig in with ladle-size spoons.

African storytellers, called *griots*, carry on an oral tradition, singing the praises of Africans, telling entertaining stories.

Beautiful dark-skinned Senegalese women, clad in colorful African fabrics, shop or work in government offices.

A huge African marketplace bustles.

Shimmying and shaking, dance troupes thrill tourists with furiously fast, acrobatic movements. They dance to the beat of drums, once used in Africa to send messages through the jungle.

French influence is apparent, too. Kiosks

A dance troupe entertains tourists at a Dakar hotel.

on street corners sell freshly baked French bread. Africans and Europeans dine on French cuisine in chic restaurants.

On Avenue Pompidou, named for a former president of France, people shop at patisseries, selecting delicate pastries, from eclairs to cake.

Meanwhile, Islam beckons, as the call to prayer issues from minarets.

"Allahu akbar!" (God is great!)

"Come to prayer!"

"Come to success!" ring muezzins' voices over loudspeakers, echoing on streets throughout Dakar.

Answering the call five times a day, Muslims prepare for prayer by performing ablution—splashing water on their faces, hands, arms, and feet. Then men in *boubous*, flowing ankle-length robes, go to local mosques, putting aside day-to-day business to bow and kneel in prayer.

All of these influences—African, French, and Islamic—converge in Dakar as a result

A Senegalese beauty

The Grand Mosque of Dakar is filled with worshipers on Friday afternoons when congregational prayer is held. Senegal is predominantly Muslim.

of a tumultuous history of commerce, the migration of African tribes that converted to Islam, and the expansion of the French empire on mainland Africa.

In 1857, the French built a fort on the African coast, and in 1862, the French commandant of Gorée laid plans for a city. A port was established at an African village of the Lebu tribe. The Lebus called their village of farmers Ndaxaru. The French came to call it Dakar.

From 1902 to 1960, Dakar was the headquarters of the government of French West Africa. Senegal—and Dakar—became independent from France on June 20, 1960. Three million Senegalese celebrated.

Meanwhile, Gorée, once the area's chief port for international commerce, was forgotten by the world's great ships. The island survived as an historical reminder and became a retreat for the busy city dwellers of Dakar.

Nearly 400 miles away, other islands also sank from memory: the Cape Verde Islands.

The powerful winds on Cape Verde can bend trees backwards.

CHAPTER FIVE

UNCOVERING MY AFRICAN PAST

In some senses, the Cape Verde Islands and Gorée are sister islands. On Cape Verde, just as on Gorée, life in the past revolved around the slave trade, which brought riches to Europeans. When slavery ended, there was hardly reason to stay.

But just as islanders remained on Gorée when slavery was abolished, islanders stayed on Cape Verde, which was much farther from the mainland.

The Cape Verdeans were able to create a new culture, a *creole* culture. They combined the *fado*, folk music of Portugal, with the exuberant rhythms of Africa. Over time, they created a new language that was a mixture of Portuguese and some African languages. They also developed their own cuisine.

Cape Verdeans settled in valleys on the islands and even inside the craters of extinct volcanoes. Farmers wrapped meat in burlap bags and roasted it in holes dug near the cone of an active volcano on Fogo (Fire) Island. My own ancestors settled at the base of a volcano, as well as in a town inside the crater of an inactive volcano on a neighboring island, Brava.

But crops would not grow, and as farmers watched rainclouds burst at sea, the soil beneath their feet turned to dust and the islands (named Cape Verde, meaning "Green Cape") turned brown. Many islanders died in a series of catastrophic famines.

Eventually, many thousands left the islands on whaleboats that were converted into

Women and girls carry heavy loads on their heads in Cape Verde today.

passenger ships. My grandparents were among the Cape Verdeans who sought a new life in America in the early 1900s.

During my childhood in New Bedford, Massachusetts, they told me stories about Cape Verde, and about relatives who still lived there. My grandparents mailed letters —and money—to them. Someday, I said, I will meet them. Not so long ago, I did.

In the village of Sumbango, on Fogo Island, I visited the oldest member of my family in a one-room, stone pile of a house whose doorway also served as a window. I had to climb through the window to meet Maria Nharita, my great-grandfather's sister.

No one was sure of her age. Some said ninety-six. She looked even older. Frail and thin, she lay on a cot and swatted flies all day, and her husband communicated with her by cupping his hands around her ears and shouting deep into her skull.

"How are you?" I asked her, through an interpreter.

"I'm alive," she guaranteed.

"Of course you are," I said. "Maria, you

are a living history book. I have come a long way to ask you some questions."

"*Say everything!*" the interpreter shouted in her ear.

"*Patience!* I can't say it all at once," she cried. "Poverty more than this I cannot explain."

"Then why didn't you leave Fogo—like my grandfather and your brothers?"

"If they didn't take me, how could I leave? I can't swim!"

She was able to trace her ancestors back to Lisbon, but not to Gorée. That was more difficult to do, since slaves kept no records, and the Portuguese slave masters did not value African heritage. Her true African identity was buried in history, hidden from her, and therefore from me.

When Maria died, she was buried in a cemetery not far from her home—the same cemetery I had searched in vain for markers or gravestones over my ancestors' graves. I was probably near them, or even walking right over them, but they were hidden from me, just as my links to mainland Africa were.

When I met Maria Nharita on Fogo, she was my oldest living relative.

American tourists at the Door of No Return look out toward the water where slave ships once docked.

CHAPTER SIX

THE OPEN DOOR

A *Time* magazine reporter who spent several years in Africa wrote:

Lacking detailed knowledge of precisely where our ancestors came from, whether they were Fon or Ashanti or Serer, African Americans have tried to adopt the continent as a whole as a place of origin. But that indiscriminate embrace poses problems of its own: Which of the hundreds of languages and cultures that flourish in Africa are we to call our own?

African Americans may never know precisely which tribes their ancestors belonged to. But places like Cape Verde and Gorée and Cape Coast Castle belong equally to all ethnic groups—Fulani, Serer, Ibo, Yoruba, and many others. They belong, in fact, to all races, because they serve as reminders of a dark chapter in human history.

Slaves landed there and then departed, and their descendants return to honor them. At a ceremony on Gorée in 1987, African Americans scattered soil from a slave cemetery in Alabama. It was like returning the spirits of kidnapped Africans to their motherland. Gorée, in a sense, was the final resting place for souls that had suffered for generations.

But Gorée is as much about the living as the dead. It is a stepping-stone for African Americans to a land rich in both culture and ancestral history. There is a feeling that Africans on Gorée today are like long-lost cousins. They may not know exactly who the ancestors of black Americans were. They may not know which tribes African Americans once belonged to, or which language their forefathers spoke. But ancestral ties have not

really been broken; they're just hidden in history.

The American tourists may be visiting for just a short time. The Africans they meet may never have left the African continent. But, in a way, the visit is like a homecoming. As Anna Faye says, there's something vaguely familiar about black Americans. They seem to be coming home to pick up something they forgot long ago and just now remembered they needed—a connection with their past.

Differences between tourists and Goréans are diminished in places like the House of Slaves. Side by side, they stand in the dungeons and imagine the horrors of slavery. A mother from Philadelphia or Detroit or Chicago senses the deep loss of a mother torn from her family in the bush of eighteenth-century Africa. And a young man from Senegal, whose own ancestors may have been sold into slavery, senses a kind of distant kinship with this American who is crying for someone she never knew.

History binds the American and the African, even if their bloodlines do not. Even if they are not really cousins.

Gorée itself was not the birthplace of most African slaves brought to America. It was a stop along the way. But it is now a door through which many people of African descent are again passing.

That door, which is redefining how African Americans relate to the motherland, now stands ajar.

The House of Slaves was built by Nicholas Pepin. Elegant curved stairways led up to the master's quarters on the upper floor.

INDEX